GIANT KILLERS, MOUNTAIN MOVERS,

and grasshoppers

Biblical Support for the Law of Attraction

Doris Rose Beerwald

Abundant Supernatural Living

Toronto, Ontario, Canada

GIANT KILLERS, MOUNTAIN MOVERS, and grasshoppers

Abundant Supernatural Living
Toronto, Ontario, Canada

Agence canadienne de l'ISBN/Canadian ISBN
Agency
Bibliothèque et Archives Canada / Library and
Archives Canada
550, boul. de la Cité, Gatineau, Qc K1A 0N4

ISBN: 978-0-9877312-0-3

—

This book is dedicated to my children. You are my greatest treasures. Jeffrey, Kayla and Kristi I love you with all my heart. Thank you for your tremendous patience, unconditional love, and unfailing support.

This book is also for those of you looking to break out of the chains of mediocrity, and to enter the higher realm of abundant supernatural living.

What then shall we say to these things? If God is for us, who can be against us? He who did not spare His own Son, but delivered Him up for us all, how shall He not with Him also freely give us all things?

Romans 8:31, 32

Contents

Part Three: Hindrances
to Receiving

Part Four: The Reality
of the Invisible

Part Five: My Desire Manifested

Part Six: Becoming Reborn

Preface

This book is in response to the popular book titled, "The Secret" by Rhonda Byrne. While researching this subject, I found that there are a lot of Christians asking if they should apply **the law of attraction** to their lives. While some Christians are advocating this practice, others are completely opposed. Since God is not the author of confusion (I Corinthians 14:33), the best thing to do would be to read "The Secret" and see if it lines up with God's word, and that is precisely what I did. I gleaned what was good advice and discarded the unscriptural teaching; in this way I did not throw out "the baby with the bathwater."

Personally, when reading "The Secret", scripture verses did come to my mind that supported what was being said, however; interwoven throughout the book are obvious **New Age concepts.** In the biographies of the contributing authors we see beliefs such as: New Spirituality, New Thought Movement, Hypnotic Writing, Metaphysics, Eastern Indigenous, and Mystical Traditions. In

"The Secret", one of the co-authors along with Ms. Byrne actually state that we are God![i] I personally find this teaching disturbing. Equally alarming is the use of "I AM". In one small paragraph "I AM" is used nine times! **I AM is God's name!**[ii]

Then Moses said to God, "Indeed, *when* I come to the children of Israel and say to them, 'The God of your fathers has sent me to you,' and they say to me, 'What is His name?' what shall I say to them?" And God said to Moses, "I AM WHO I AM." And He said, "Thus you shall say to the children of Israel, 'I AM has sent me to you.' "
Exodus 3:13, 14

The use of "I AM" has a New Age connotation to it in that its philosophy preaches that we are **GOD**. We can only be one with God through Jesus Christ our Lord (John 17:11), **but we are not God.**
My intention here is to show which beliefs in Ms. Byrne's book line up with scripture and which ones do not, and *my prayer for you is that by reading these words you will be encouraged, strengthened,*

empowered, and inspired, but most importantly—<u>not misled!</u>

I want you woven into a tapestry of love, in touch with everything there is to know of God. Then you will have minds confident and at rest, focused on Christ, God's great mystery. All the richest treasures of wisdom and knowledge are embedded in that mystery and nowhere else. And we've been shown the mystery! I'm telling you this because I don't want anyone leading you off on some wild-goose chase, after other so-called mysteries, or "the Secret."
Colossians 2:2-4 (The Message)

The only way to recognize false teaching is through faithfully and consistently studying the bible, and intimately fellowshipping with the Lord.

Introduction

The main theme in "The Secret" stresses the magnitude of our thought life. We are repeatedly told our thoughts are energy, that they are important, and they have the power to direct our life's course. This concept is called **the law of attraction** and is defined as **like attracts like**. We have the choice to either attract good or bad into our lives by virtue of our thoughts.

In Hebrews 11:1, The New Living Translation defines faith as: **The confident assurance that what we hope for is going to happen. It is the evidence of things we cannot see.** Faith believes for the best, while negative faith or fear believes for the worst. Scripture does tell us to think right and good thoughts as demonstrated by the following verses.

For as he thinks in his heart, so is he. Proverbs 23:7a

"Become what you believe." Matthew 9:29 (The Message)

The preceding verses are quite clear; we are or become what we think. According to the bible we are to think on good and positive things. I like how the New Living Translation tells us to **fix** our thoughts on what is good.

Fix your thoughts on what is true and honorable and right. Think about things that are pure and lovely and admirable. Think about things that are excellent and worthy of praise.
Philippians 4:8b (NLT)

If our thoughts do not have influence, why then, would the bible tell us to meditate on positive things? Does positive thinking really create a good result? Conversely, does negative thinking actually produce a bad outcome? Is our life's course, in fact, impacted by our thoughts? According to Proverbs 4:23 our thoughts play a huge role in the direction our life takes. The New Living Translation declares: **Above all else, guard your heart, for it affects everything you do.** Let us now examine the scriptures to see how important our thoughts really are.

PART ONE

Bible Personalities and What Their Lives Teach Us

Fearful Job

Be sober, be vigilant; because your adversary the devil walks about like a roaring lion, seeking whom he may devour.
I Peter 5:8

Job feared God and his reverential fear was very good, but **Job was also full of fear which was exceedingly detrimental**. His ten sons always celebrated their birthdays. He regularly offered sacrifices on behalf of his children to God just in case they sinned during their celebrations.

One day Satan showed up before God. He'd been wandering the earth, [probably], looking for his next victim. Like a pleased father, God happily extolled all of Job's virtues to the devil. Satan immediately went on the offence and accused God of completely protecting and blessing Job. Satan was positive that if God took away all the good things from Job's life that Job would curse God. Therefore, at the devil's insistence, God allowed Job's livelihood, family and health to be destroyed. Job's immediate response to the calamity was:

For the thing I greatly feared has come upon me, And what I dreaded has happened to me.
Job 3:25

Job had a picture of calamity coming upon his family which he played over and over in his mind. Fear and dread consumed Job's life. What a terrible way to live. Job saw destruction coming and it came to pass. This is a tremendous example of the power negative thinking fueled by the spirit of fear.

Why did God allow Satan to all but destroy Job? Job was a good man. God referred to Job as upright and blameless (Job 2:3). God allowed Job to suffer in order to do a work in his life. The transformation occurred after Job had a personal encounter with The Living God. Previous to that encounter Job knew of God but **he did not know God**. **Job was also full of fear,** and debilitating fear is not of God.

For God has not given us a spirit of fear, but of power and love and of a sound mind.
II Timothy 1:7

There is another valuable lesson to be learnt here. Throughout his hellacious ordeal, even though greatly perplexed, Job did not blaspheme God but kept his integrity. If Job had listened to his wife who told him to curse God and die, that would have been the end of Job. Job would have missed out on the great life God still had in store for him.

You may be completely bewildered by your circumstances, but don't you dare give up. God still has an amazing life planned for you! Nothing takes God by surprise; he is still on the throne. God is large and in charge and he will give you double for your trouble. After all, that's what he did for Job, and if he did it for Job, he will do it for you because God does not show partiality (Acts 10:34).

For I know the thoughts that I think toward you, says the Lord, thoughts of

peace and not of evil, to give you a future and a hope.
Jeremiah 29:11

After his deliverance, Job was a new man with a renewed mind. His mind was no longer sick; his mind was sound. Fear took flight, the devil shut up and left, and faith moved in. God not only restored Job's losses but gave him twice as much as he had before. God blessed him with health, and one hundred and forty more years of life. Job not only became a father again, but also a grandfather, a great grandfather and a great, great grandfather.

After examining Job's life we can indeed see that your thought life can direct your life's course. It is wonderful to see how much God wants not only prosper and bless you, but make you whole; he may even use the devil to accomplish his purposes.

Beloved, I pray that you may prosper in all things and be in health, just as your soul prospers.
III John 2

Faithful Abraham

He did not waver at the promises of God through unbelief, but was strengthened in faith, giving glory to God, and being fully convinced that what He had promised He was also able to perform.
Romans 4:20, 21

At the age of seventy-five Abram was told by God that he would be the father of a great nation. To help Abram hold on to the promise, God told him to look toward heaven and count the stars (if he was able); his descendants would be as the stars in the sky (Genesis 15:5). To help Abram stay encouraged for when the stars were not visible, God gave another promise to Abram in stating that his descendents would be as the dust of the earth (Genesis 13:16).

"The Secret" instructs us to use a vision board.[iii] It is especially advantageous to write down or make pictures of your goals. Your chances of accomplishing your dreams improve dramatically when you continually remind yourself of them.

The stars in the sky and the dust of the earth were Abram's vision boards; one for the day and one for the night.

At the age of ninety nine Abram's name which means high father was changed by God to Abraham. Abraham means father of a great multitude. Likewise Sarai's name was changed to Sarah. The meaning of Sarai is my princess, but Sarah means princess of the multitude.

Finally, after twenty-five years of waiting for the promise, Isaac was born to one hundred year old Abraham and ninety year old Sarah.

"If you can believe, all things are possible to him who believes."
Mark 9:23b

Like most couples, Abraham and Sarah wanted children or at least an heir. It took a long time, steadfast faith and courage [I mention courage here because I imagine the people in the community, in which Abraham and Sarah lived, probably ridiculed them as they called themselves by their new names], but Abraham and

Sarah did not give up and quit, therefore; the promise came to pass.

Now faith is the substance of things hoped for, the evidence of things not seen.
Hebrews 11:1

Faith not only hears (God telling Abraham he would be the father of a great multitude) and sees, (God showing Abraham the stars in the sky and the dust of the earth), but faith also speaks (Abraham and Sarah professing they were the parents of a great multitude by using their new names). This is a remarkable account of how the law of attraction operates.

As free will agents, suppose Abraham and Sarah decided not to believe God because they were too old, and it was impossible in the natural to have a child, let alone be parents to a great nation. God would have not used them and they would have died childless. Still, God's sovereign plan would not have been thwarted; the child of promise, I believe, would have been born to another obedient couple.

If you say no to God he will still love you but, his plan will go forward and he will use someone else (Ester 4:14).

Creative Jacob

"For with God nothing will be impossible."
Luke 1:37

After Jacob had worked for his Uncle Laban for twenty years, it was time for payday! The deal was that Jacob would get all the speckled and spotted sheep, every dark colored lamb, and every speckled and spotted goat (Genesis 30:32). To keep Jacob from prospering, Jacob's uncle had all of the animals that were supposed to be Jacob's removed and placed under the care of his sons. He also distanced himself and the animals from Jacob by three days journey. Jacob was left to tend Laban's solid colored flocks. In the natural the animals would produce more solid colored animals, but that did not deter Jacob. He simply rolled up his sleeves and went to work.

For as the body without the spirit is dead, so faith without works is dead also.
James 2:26

Earlier I mentioned that faith hears, sees, and speaks, but that is not all; faith also requires action. Jacob took action. He took fresh branches from poplar, almond, and chestnut trees, and stripped some of the bark off of them so that the branches looked like they had white patches on them. He then placed these branches in front of the animals' watering troughs. When the animals mated in front of the branches, they produced speckled and spotted offspring. I don't think a top of his or her class geneticist could have pulled that off!

Jacob stared at his vision board of branches, and saw his speckled and spotted flocks. The animals mated and produced speckled, spotted, and mottled offspring. Jacob did what was humanly possible, and the Holy Spirit went to work and did the impossible.

"If you have faith as a mustard seed, you will say to this mountain, 'Move from here to there', and it will move; and nothing will be impossible for you."
Matthew 17:20

Joseph the Dreamer

For the vision is yet for an appointed time; But at the end it will speak, and it will not lie.
Habakkuk 2:3

Joseph was Jacob's favorite son and this favoritism did not fair well with his brothers. One day Jacob gave Joseph a coat of many colors. This gift caused Joseph's brothers to become even more hateful and jealous. Joseph also dreamed that his brothers' bundles of grain all bowed down to Joseph's bundle of grain which he eagerly shared with them. This unwelcome news nearly drove his brothers to insanity, but Joseph kept right on dreaming and sharing. The next dream was about the sun, the moon, and eleven stars bowing down to Joseph. This time Joseph's father even rebuked him, although he knew in his heart, Joseph was destined for greatness (Genesis 37:11).

Joseph's recounting of his dreams to his brothers did drive them to insanity. They already felt second rate and the thought of Joseph lording over them sent them over the edge. Although they stopped short of murder, they did sell their seventeen year old brother into slavery.

When you discover God's will for your life, you are eager to fulfill it. Sadly though, as you share with people and step out in faith, you will very quickly find out that not everyone is going to support you. In fact, you will likely be persecuted and ridiculed, but don't be surprised if some of those who go against you are your friends and family. **It may be easier to just give up and go along with them, but don't you let these people talk you out of your dream(s).**

Getting back to the story of Joseph, we find that he was bought by Potiphar, an officer of Pharaoh. Joseph, however; quickly gained favor with his master. This arrangement did not last very long for the young, handsome, and well built Joseph as Potiphar's wife made advances toward him. When Joseph brushed off her advances, this scorned woman accused Joseph of attempted rape. Joseph was quickly thrown into prison.

Sometimes doing the right thing makes your situation worse [for a season], but had Joseph given into temptation he may [very well] not have fulfilled his destiny. Joseph continued to be his best in prison, and again quickly gained favor with the head jailer.

Joseph spent the next thirteen years in jail. How did he survive and not grow bitter? God gave Joseph those dreams to sustain him. Joseph believed he was destined for greatness even when things looked hopeless. **Joseph was a prisoner of hope**. Joseph kept the faith, and God made a way for Joseph to finally be set free by giving him a gift; this gift was the ability to interpret dreams. Joseph used his gift to interpret Pharaoh's disturbing dreams and was able to step into his destiny (Genesis 41:40).

"As for you also, because of the blood of your covenant, I will set your prisoners free from the waterless pit. Return to the stronghold, you prisoners of hope. Even today I

---

declare that I will restore double to you."
Zechariah 9:11, 12

Are you a prisoner of hope? The bible tells us to rest in hope (Acts 2:26), and not in despair. Like Joseph, are you using the gift God that gave you? If not, then stir it up (II Timothy 1:6)! How would you feel if you gave someone you love a present and they just tossed it aside? You would probably feel angry and hurt. Why should God feel any different if we just ignore or misuse the gifts and talents He bestows upon us? Do not waste your gift, but use it instead to fulfill God's will for your life.

Patient David

King Saul displeased God by his unlawful sacrifice, and as a consequence God rejected Saul as king. God told Samuel the Prophet to go to Bethlehem and anoint one of Jesse's sons. Jesse lined up seven of his sons, but the Lord did not choose them. Samuel had to ask Jesse if he had another son. Jesse admitted he had a younger son named David who was tending the sheep, and I imagine how awkward it must have been for Jesse to send for David.

When David arrived Samuel was instructed by the Lord to anoint David as King. I love how God more than not uses **the most unlikely people**. If you fall into that category, **rejoice!** God has something special for you.

But the Lord said to Samuel, "Do not look at his appearance or at the height of his stature, because I have refused him (Eliab, Jesse's oldest son). For *the* **Lord** *does* **not** *see* **as a man sees; for the man looks at the out-ward**

appearance, but the Lord looks at the heart."
I Samuel 16:7
The addition of text in parentheses within the scripture quotation is mine; it is for the purpose of clarification.

David did not step into his role as king immediately. David was anointed when he was a youth, but he did not become King of Israel until he was thirty years old. He patiently waited until the death of King Saul. David had, on two occasions, opportunity to kill King Saul (I Samuel chapters 24:11 & 26:23), but he refused even though King Saul was trying to kill him. The point I'm trying to make here is that sometimes you take action, and sometimes you wait patiently on the Lord, and the only way to determine that is through prayer and spending time in his presence.

David spent over ten years waiting to step into his destiny, but he spent that time with the Lord, which gave him the strength to endure. David, from time to time, got discouraged and understandably so, but he always encouraged himself in the Lord. Samuel also spoke powerful words over David and anointed him with oil. That moment in time was forever **etched** in David's memory. I believe, in the difficult times, he heard Samuel's prophetic words, felt the prophet anointing him with oil all over again, and that recollection enabled David to not give up.

Wait on the Lord; Be of good courage, And he shall strengthen your heart; Wait, I say, on the Lord!
Psalm 27:14

Caleb the Visionary

and they (Joshua and Caleb) spoke to all the congregation of the children of Israel, saying: "The land we passed through to spy out is an exceedingly good land. If the Lord delights in us, then He will bring us into this land and give it to us, a land which flows with milk and honey."
Numbers 14:7, 8
The addition of text in parentheses within the scripture quotation is mine; it is for the purpose of clarification.

Caleb was forty-five years old when, along with Joshua, he made the above statement. Unfortunately, after searching out the land, the other ten spies brought back a negative report. All twelve spies saw giants in the land, but the ten spies, with the negative report, saw themselves as grasshoppers (Numbers 13:33), and convinced the children of Israel that they could not possess the land. After witnessing all of God's miracles, it is astonishing that the children of Israel refused to enter the Promised Land, but the gloomy report melted their hearts.

They started complaining and actually wanted to return to their former life of slavery in Egypt. It was like slapping God in the face. Instead of trusting in God and having a giant killer mentality, they chose to complain, adopted a grasshopper mindset, and sadly perished in the desert. I can only imagine how frustrated Joshua and Caleb felt when they were overruled, and forced to wander in the desert for forty years.

If you can avoid it, do not be involved with pessimistic people; they can delay God's best for you for a long time. If you are stuck with negative people, find some Joshuas and Calebs to associate with, or you yourself be like Joshua and Caleb.

If you are constantly grumbling, **_watch out_**, you will not likely fulfill God's will for your life because God hates complaining. Remember God threatened to disinherit and strike the Israelites with a pandemic, and make a greater nation starting all over again with Moses (Numbers 14:12). It was only Moses' humility and intercession which saved them from immediate destruction (verse 19).

Eventually though, that whole generation with the exception of Joshua and Caleb died in the wilderness.

Even though Caleb, along with Joshua, was forced to wander in the desert, he had a picture of Mount Hebron, in the Promised Land, in his heart. I believe he saw himself living there in the mist of his nomadic existence. Caleb was eighty-five years old when he boldly asked for Mount Hebron for his inheritance. This octogenarian said he felt as good at eighty-five years old as he did when he was forty years old. God did sustain Caleb, but Caleb's trust in God and positive outlook helped Caleb to stay strong and healthy.

"Now therefore, give me this mountain of which the Lord spoke of in that day... ." And Joshua blessed him, and gave Hebron to Caleb the son of Jephunneh as an inheritance.
Joshua 14:12, 13

Stay in faith, keep believing and expecting. Stop listening to the nay Sayers, and never say you are too old to accomplish what has God put in your heart. **It's your dream and no one else's.**

Highly Esteemed Ester

"The 'Secret" teaches us that we are Masters of the Universe, and as masters, we can command the Universe to do our bidding. To demonstrate this concept more easily, the allegory of Aladdin and his lamp is used to describe the process of us receiving whatever we desire. The Genie always says, **"Your wish is my command!"**[iv]

The co-authors of "The Secret" have reduced God to a Genie, and elevated humanity to Godhood. This is false New Age teaching. We are created beings (Romans 9:20) and cannot be God. God is The Potter and we are the clay (verse 21). In Romans 3:23, the bible says all have sinned and fall short of the glory of God. The following statements describe some of the attributes and accomplishments of God. God is omnipotent (all-powerful), omniscient (all-knowing), and omnipresent (always present everywhere). God is an all-consuming fire. God is sovereign. God is holy. God is the creator of the universe and everything in it. God is from everlasting to everlasting. God is our Father. God is merciful. God is (unconditional) love. Can we boost of any of the above traits and deeds? I don't think so. **God is The Master!**

You can find God's resume in the book of Job in chapters 38 through to 41. His works are pretty impressive and cannot be matched by any man.

There is, however; another way of looking at the statement, "Your wish is my command, and it has to do with having favor with the king. Upon learning of the plot to destroy her people, Queen Ester wisely prepared for her impending perilous visit with the king by fasting with her maids for three days. She also instructed her Uncle Mordecai to tell the Jews to fast for her. We have no mention of Queen Ester telling anyone to pray along with the fasting. There was, however; a really good reason for all of this. Queen Ester was undercover! She was hiding the fact that she was Jewish from the entire palace. If she had prayed openly to Jehovah with her maids, she would have been immediately reported to the King. This in turn would have led her to prompt execution. I believe all of the Jews prayed and fasted during this time, but Queen Ester prayed in secret.

"Behold, I send you out as sheep in the midst of wolves. Therefore be wise as serpents and harmless as doves."
Matthew 10:16

Fasting and praying make for a very powerful team. In Mark 9:29 Jesus states, **"This kind can come out by nothing but prayer and fasting."** This potent combination of fasting and the prayers of the Jewish people is what broke the murderous demonic stronghold over them, and gave Queen Ester favor with the King. When Queen Ester appeared before her King, he esteemed her highly and offered her up to half his kingdom.

She did not present her request immediately, but invited the king and Haman, his highest ranking official, to dinner. This act is symbolic of fellowshipping with the Lord. We get so busy with our petitions, we forget to spend time with God, and simply enjoy his presence.

After Queen Ester had spent time with her king, he again offered her up to half his kingdom. Queen Ester revealed Haman's evil plot to destroy her and her people to King Ahasuerus. She interceded for herself and her people, and as a result, the Jews were spared and their enemies were slaughtered.

Queen Ester was given the estate of her archenemy, Haman. This was poetic justice. Highly favored Queen Ester was showered with unprecedented favor and grace by the king.

The king asked Queen Ester, "What else do you want? Name it and it's yours. Your wish is my command." Ester 9:12 (The Message)

Just as King Ahasuerus loved Ester deeply and was eager to bless her, God loves us with tremendous intensity and wants to richly bless us as well. By following Queen Ester's example, we too can have favor with our Lord, and have our wishes and desires become **his command.**

Gideon's Transformation

Gideon perceived himself as an individual of very little worth. He stated his clan was the weakest, and that he was the least in his father's house. Just like his ancestors who perished in the desert, Gideon had a "grasshopper mentality". He was very fearful, as demonstrated by the fact, that he was threshing wheat in the winepress out of sight of the Midianites. And yet, God called Gideon a mighty man of valor (Judges 6:12).

Once Gideon changed his thinking and saw himself as God saw him—"a mighty man of valor" and that God was with him, he was able to fulfill his destiny. Gideon went on to subdue his enemies, [the innumerable Midianite army] with only three hundred men (Judges 7:22).

It is time to stop listening to the Accuser of the Brethren (Revelation 12:10); get out of the winepress into the open, and start listening to and agreeing with what God says about you:

Yet in all things we are more than conquerors through Him who loved us. Romans 8:37

PART TWO

God's Sovereignty and Our Participation

The Existence of Evil

What "The Secret" fails to mention is the existence of evil. The universe is portrayed as a friendly place, but if something does go wrong, we are told that it is our own fault because we attracted the calamity through our thinking.

In "The Secret" there is mention of having a car accident because you attracted it,[v] and I suppose if you are completely convinced of being in a wreck [prophesying it day and night], you likely will bring the occasion to pass. I always pray for traveling mercies, not because I expect to be in a collision, but because I know I share the road with drunks, stoners, speeders, and careless drivers. And let's not forget; the devil likes nothing better than to steal, kill, and destroy (John 10:10).

It is merely not just our thinking that attracts calamity, but disobedience to God's commands. According to Deuteronomy 28 defying The Lord's rules will result in curses.

After God finished the creation process, he stated that everything was very good, and he gave Adam and Eve dominion over the earth. Tragically Adam and Eve handed over their authority to Satan. As a result, sin and corruption entered the world. Because of the fall of humanity, this law of attraction business is not as simplistic as these New Ages proponents would have us to believe.

"These things I have spoken to you, that in Me you may have peace. In the world you will have tribulation; but be of good cheer, I have overcome the world."
John 16:33

Earlier I mention how Job contributed to his calamity by his evil forebodings, and I still adhere to my opinion; however, there times when you will be tested regardless of how positive you are. Where God seemingly recommended Job to the devil to be tested by him, knowing Job would eventually profit from his trials, the devil specifically asked for Peter. Peter does not strike me as a pessimistic individual. When Jesus spoke of his impending death and resurrection, Peter rebuked him and told Jesus that was not going to happen. Peter was a very impulsive man who quite often spoke without thinking. Sometimes I wonder if he thought at all. To his credit though, Peter was the first to declare Jesus as the Messiah, and to walk on water.

Even though Peter promptly flunked his trial by Satan, and denied the Lord Jesus three times, he went on to redeem himself by being the first of the disciples to enter the empty tomb (Luke 24:12), and by preaching the first sermon resulting in three thousand souls being saved (Acts 2:41).

Trials will come no matter how positive we are. Our job is to remain joyful and to totally trust in the Father.

My brethren, count it all joy when you fall into various trials, knowing that the testing of your faith produces patience. But let patience have its perfect work, that you may be perfect and complete, lacking nothing.
James 1:2-4

God is Sovereign

"The Secret" claims that we can have whatever we want. We just have to ask for it, imagine it, believe it, feel it, and it will be ours. I believe the devil thinks positive. He has been after the top job practically from the beginning. The following verses come across as extremely optimistic:

For you (Lucifer) have said in your heart:
'I will ascend into heaven,
I will exalt my throne above the stars of God;
I will also sit on the mount of the congregation
On the farthest sides of the north;
I will ascend above the heights of the clouds,
I will be like the Most High.'
Isaiah 14:13, 14
The addition of text in parentheses within the scripture quotations is mine; it is for the purpose of clarification.

That's a lot of I wills. This extremely conniving beast went on the persuade one third of the angels to rebel against God (Revelation 12:4). This coup attempt got Satan thrown out of the third heaven. He did not ascend, instead he descended. Satan, however; still believes he will win the final battle. The devil can think positive, believe, speak, strive, battle all he wants, but Satan's ultimate destiny is in the lake of fire (Revelation 20:10)!

Contrast now, Satan's pride and arrogance with Jesus' humility and love for The Father. Suffering under extreme stress as evidenced by sweating blood, Jesus was certainly dreading going to the cross, however; he was ready and willing to do God's will.

And He said, "Abba, Father, all things are possible for You. Take this cup away from Me; nevertheless, not what I will, but what You will."
Mark 14:36

Likewise you should strive to do God's will. He created you; He has a perfect plan for your life, and He knows what's best for you. Even though we have free will, God is sovereign. When it comes to the grand scheme of things, he always gets the final word.

Resistance is Not Futile

Therefore submit to God. Resist the devil and he will flee from you.
James 4:7

We are told in "The Secret" that what we resist persists.[vi] This is contrary to the scriptures. If, in the Garden of Eden, Eve would have resisted the devil, the fall of humanity would have not happened. If we replace the word resist with its antonym, we have the phrase "what we give in to persists." This phrase is logical and true.

Saying what we resist persist is like saying to the drug addict give in to your temptation. The drug addict must resist the temptation to do the drug if he or she is to be set free from it.

Your resistance, however; must be balanced. You must resist your temptation, but your thoughts cannot be consumed with only the negative aspect of your problem. This would be very energy draining. You must also see yourself free of your difficult situation, and believe all things are possible with God's help.

I can do all things through Christ who strengthens me.
Philippians 4:13

God's Perfect Will is the Better Way

Wait on the Lord; Be of good courage, And he shall strengthen your heart; Wait, I say, on the Lord! Psalm 27:14

Sarai and Abram were told they were going to have a son. Instead of waiting for God's perfect timing, they took matters into their own hands and had Abram impregnate Sarai's servant, Hagar, at Sarai's suggestion. Bad idea! In those days when a woman could not conceive, she was made to feel less of a woman, and as soon a Hagar became pregnant she began treating Sarai with disdain. Sarai quickly blamed Abram (can't you men do anything right?—just kidding!), but Abram wisely let Sarai handle the problem. After all he was in enough trouble already!

Soon after, Hagar gave birth to Ishmael, and the tension between Sarai and Hagar continued. Sarai never did accept Ishmael, even though the plan was for her to have a child through Hagar. I guess it seemed like a good idea to her at the time.

It would be another fourteen years before Isaac finally arrived, but the day ultimately came. What a joyous time! The miracle had come to pass. No one was laughing at Abraham and Sarah. They were laughing with them. No one was saying they were crazy. God delivered—pun intended! Are people laughing at you? Just follow your heart, and let them laugh. One day they will be laughing with you!

Once Isaac was weaned, Abraham decided to throw a party to celebrate, but what should have been a happy occasion became a heartbreaking one [especially for Abraham]. When Sarah saw Hagar and Ishmael teasing Isaac, she demanded that Abraham send them away. Let this be a lesson for all you men out there; one woman is enough! With great anguish, Abraham sent Hagar and his beloved boy, Ishmael, away so peace could be restored in the family.

Because God is a loving God, he promised to bless Ishmael and make him a great nation for Abraham's sake (Genesis 17:20).

Abraham and Sarah should have waited for God's perfect timing, but they went ahead with their own strategy. Had Abraham and Sarah waited on God instead of implementing their own scheme, they would have saved themselves a tremendous amount of grief. Taking matters into their own hands caused them a lot of heartache. The consequences of Abraham's and Sarah's actions have produced the greatest sibling rivalry that continues to this day.

You do not want your actions bringing you sorrow, and possibly affecting future generations in a negative way. Praying and screening your desires through scripture will keep you on the right track. You will know if your petition or action is right because you will have peace in your heart.

Be anxious for nothing, but in everything by prayer and supplication, with thanksgiving, let your requests be

made known to God; and the peace of God, which surpasses all understanding, will guard your hearts and minds through Christ Jesus. Philippians 4:6. 7

As Jesus did in the Garden of Gethsemane, pray for God's will to be done in your life. Give birth to an Isaac, which represents God's perfect will as opposed to giving birth to an Ishmael, which represents God's permissive will. After all Psalms 18:30 declares God's way is perfect.

Show Gratitude

Giving thanks always for all things to God the Father in the name of our Lord Jesus Christ.
Ephesians 5:20

"The Secret" calls gratitude a powerful process, and persuades us to have an "attitude of gratitude."[vii] This is **GREAT ADVICE**, and has the potential to bring the miraculous into your life. The following paragraph demonstrates this principle.

After Paul and Silas were beaten, and thrown into the inner prison, [their feet secured in stocks], they were found praying and singing hymns to God. They were **not grumbling** to God, "Is this the thanks we get for preaching the gospel?" On the contrary, they were praising and worshipping him.

Suddenly an earthquake caused all the prison doors to be opened, and the prisoners' chains to be loosed (Acts 16:23-26). Suppose Paul and Silas had been complaining about their unjust ordeal. Would they have gotten out of prison that night? Would the Philippian jailer and his family have gotten saved? I don't believe so. But, because Paul and Silas offered up praise and not protest, God performed a miracle on their behalf.

And we know that all things work together for good to those who love God, to those who are called according to his purpose.
Romans 8:28

God's plans for us are for good and not for evil (Jeremiah 29:11). When we complain, we disrupt his perfect plans, not only for our life, but we also upset the lives of those around us. This is one reason why God hates our whining so much. The Israelites spent forty years, in the desert, making an eleven day trip because of their complaining and disobedience. That whole generation that grieved God so much, with the exception of Caleb and Joshua, never made it into the Promised Land, but died in the desert (Numbers 14:26-38).

A number of years ago, my daughter had a dream. One morning she said, "Mommy, I had a dream that you died in the wilderness." That really shook me to the core. Many times I prayed, "God don't let me die in the wilderness." It took me a long time to realize what the dream signified. What it meant was, if I kept on complaining, and I was really "good" at it, that I would never really obtain abundant life. In other words, I would never enter the Promised Land. Since I do want abundant life, I am now practicing being thankful. I urge you to do the same.

Enter into His gates with thanksgiving, And into His courts with praise. Be thankful to Him, *and bless* His name. Psalm 100:4

In "The Power" [the sequel to "The Secret"] gratitude is described as the Great Multiplier.[viii] Before the feeding of the five thousand (John 6:9-13), Jesus lifted up the five barley loaves and the two small fish to heaven and **gave thanks**. Consequently, the food was multiplied and all the people were fed. If Jesus himself showed gratitude, how much more

should we?   Bring more blessings into
your life by being thankful!

Make a Joyful Noise

A merry heart does good, like medicine, But a broken spirit dries the bones.
Proverbs 17:2

In "The Secret" we are told that laughter is the best medicine.[ix] This statement is supported by the above scripture. Since laughter is like medicine, then take your medicine daily. Read a funny book or watch a funny movie. If you can not find anything funny, then laugh on purpose. Find someone to laugh with. The infectious nature of laughter will keep you and company laughing for quite some time.

Not only is laughter good for you but it will make you a more attractive person. People will be drawn to you because you are fun to be around. Is that not better that having a scowl on your face, and pushing people away?

Give Cheerfully

"Give, and it will be given to you: good measure, pressed down, shaken together, and running over... ."
Luke 6:38

Giving to get is motivated by greed. We should give out of a cheerful (II Corinthians 9:7) and pure heart without expecting anything in return. But because God put the sowing and reaping principle into place (Galatians 6:7), giving will always produce a harvest in your life. Whatever you have need of, is what you give away. Do not hoard it. Instead, plant it like a seed. Water it with your prayers. Believe, have patience and you will receive.

The following account demonstrates the sowing and reaping law in action. Because of a drought in the land, the widow at Zarephath had only enough flour and oil to make a small meal. According to the widow, it was going to be the last meal for her and her son before they starved. Elijah the Prophet asked the widow to make him a small biscuit first, and then use what was left of the oil and flour to feed herself and her son. The widow complied with Elijah's request. As a result, God blessed the widow for her giving, so that she, her son, and Elijah were able to eat for many days, and the oil and flour did not run out until the drought ended.

As most people usually are, I was in prayer about finances. Suddenly, in a vision, I saw the most beautiful and gentle hands. They exuded such kindness. They were, of course, God's hands. As I watched, these same gentle hands scooped up what looked like golden, shimmering sand and then proceeded to pour this shimmering sand out of heaven. I immediately knew, in my spirit, these were many blessings. The area containing the blessings was vast— enough for all. This vision illuminates the scripture: **"Bring all the tithes into the storehouse, That there may be food in My house, And prove (test) Me now in this," Says the Lord of hosts "If I will not open for you the windows of heaven and pour out for you *such***

blessing **That** *there will not be room* **enough** *to receive it."*
Malachi 3:10
The addition of text in parentheses within the scripture quotation is mine; it is for the purpose of clarification.

We are not to test God (Luke 4:12), but we are given permission to test Him in the area of our finances, specifically tithing. If we tithe, God promises not only to pour out such blessing that cannot be contained, but that he will rebuke the devourer (Malachi 3:11) so that he [the devil] cannot steal the abundant life God has in store for us.

Do Not Love Money

Rhonda Byrne advises us to love money.[x] She quotes the bible numerous times in her book, but this particular statement is totally against biblical principles. The bible clearly states that the **LOVE** of money is a root of all kinds of evil which brings sorrow. (I Timothy 6:10). From the beginning of time, people have perpetrated all kinds of unimaginable acts of evil for money.

Even though Ms. Byrne tells us to love money, I'm pretty sure she's not advocating that we harm one another in order to receive it. In her next book, called "The Power", she states," There is one rule with money: You can never put money ahead of love."[xi] Besides, an abundance of money is no guarantee of true wealth anyway. There are many rich people who are miserable. In Proverbs 10:22, the bible says, **"The blessing of The Lord makes one rich, And He adds no sorrow with it."**

Prospering is so much more that just having a lot of money. It's about having a rich relationship with God, and with the people in your life. It's about having your physical and mental health. If you are sick and lonely you are not going to enjoy the money anyway. A healthy well-balanced life is a rich life.

Beloved, I pray that you may prosper in all things and be in health, just as your soul prospers.
III John 2

The word prospers means to thrive or flourish. The preceding verse tells us that the course of your life and health is determined by the condition of your soul. And the condition of your soul is determined by your thoughts. If you want an abundant life, it has to come from the inside.

PART THREE

Hindrances to Receiving

Vague Prayers

"Therefore I say to you, whatever things you ask when you pray, believe that you receive *them*, and you will have *them*."
Mark 11:24

Vague prayers rarely produce results. Your prayers must be specific. When Jacob believed for the increase of his herds, he wasn't just envisioning sheep, goats, and lambs; he was envisioning spotted and speckled sheep and goats, and brown lambs. In his thoughts, he was being clear and specific about what kind of animals he wanted, and he went through what seemed like a very outrageous process to acquire them (Genesis 30:37-42).

Make your requests specific, just like a title-deed. A title-deed is very detailed. It contains the date, the names, signatures, and addresses of the parties involved. The terms are outlined in this legal document as well a description of the property.

You may find it helpful to make up a detailed document of your desire. Even if this sounds like a bizarre thing to do, read your "title-deed" aloud everyday thankfully proclaiming that whatever you are believing for is yours until your prayer is answered or your desire is made visible.

If an indistinct prayer is answered, it can be attributed to coincidence. A clear-cut or precise prayer is that is answered is difficult for the unbeliever to dismiss!

Doubt, Worry, and Indecision

But when you ask him, be sure that you really expect him to answer, for a doubtful mind is as unsettled as a wave of the sea that is driven and tossed by the wind. People like that should not expect to receive anything from the Lord. They can't make up their minds. They waver back and forth in everything they do.
James 1:6-8 (NLT)

This verse pertains to people who constantly contradict themselves. They say one thing, but they do the opposite. Their thoughts, words, and actions are not in harmony with each other, but rather oppose one another.

In mathematics positive and negative numbers cancel each other out. For example: Positive two plus negative two equals zero. Likewise, when your thoughts, words, and actions are in disagreement with one another, they cancel each other out, and you wind up with nothing.

Worry is another hindrance. It partners with fear and saps all your energy; energy you could be using in accomplishing your goals.
Stop replaying those time-wasting worst-case scenarios in your head and start believing for the best and not the worst.

"Give your entire attention to what God is doing right now, and don't get worked up about what may or may not happen tomorrow. God will help you deal with whatever hard things come up when the time comes."
Matthew 6:34 (The Message)

Indecision will also keep you from receiving because you are sending mixed signals. You must decide on what you want, and **focus** on it with **laser precision**. Stop constantly changing your mind!

I like the example of the single artist, given in "The Secret", who was told to paint a picture of the relationship he wanted. Instead of painting pictures of the same woman turning away from him, he was to a picture of being involved in a romantic relationship. The strategy worked and he was married one year later.[xii]

Because you are only human, doubts will creep into your thought life. You must not allow them to take root. A beautiful garden needs to be weeded regularly. If the weeds are left unchecked, they will choke out the flowers and take over. Think of your positive thoughts as beautiful flowers and see your negative thoughts as weeds. As soon as a negative thought creeps in, imagine yanking it out by the root and throwing it into the compost heap. Like unwelcome weeds, do not let your bad thoughts take root.

Do not condemn yourself, in a moment of weakness, if you have a pessimistic thought. Repent and promptly deal with it, and press forward. Jesus will not abandon you. Remember how gracious and patient he was with Doubting Thomas (John 20:27-29).

A Lack of Action

There are times when you must take action and participate in answer to your prayers. After all, the bible does say that faith without works is dead (James 2:20). Jacob cut up branches and stripped bark; and with the Holy Spirit's help, increased his herds. Caleb claimed his mountain and drove out the giants. After his attitude adjustment, Gideon subdued his enemies.

Whatever you want to aspire to, you are going to have to **work** at it. I don't mean to sound condescending here, but if you, for example, want to become a doctor, you are going to have to work at becoming a doctor. Praying, but lying around and watching ER is not going to do it for you. Similarly, if you are talking about going into ministry, ask yourself, "What am I doing to prepare myself?" and then take the necessary steps that will get you to your destination.

God ordained work, and he expects you to do your part. Shortly after God created Adam, he gave him a job. Adam's job was to tend the garden in Eden (Genesis 2:15). Not working will quickly lead to poverty, and you simply cannot just rely on the law of attraction without good old fashioned work to make your dreams come true.

Sloth makes you poor; diligence brings wealth.
Proverbs 10:4 (The Message)

However, sometimes praying and waiting on the Lord is exactly what you will have to do. How then, do you know when you should go ahead with your plans, and when you should wait on the Lord? You spend time with God just like David. You declare for God's will to be done in your life. You **pray** and you **listen**. You continue to **work** and **do your best** while you are waiting on the Lord. You ask for wisdom, and God will freely give (James 1:5). You start renewing your mind by thinking right thoughts. As you go through this process of renewing your mind, you will gain a greater sense of clarity (Romans 12:2). In due course, you will have a knowing in your spirit as too as to what plan of action you are to take because you will have peace in your heart (Philippians 4:7).

Faithlessness

But without faith it is impossible to please *Him*, for he who comes to God must believe that He is, and *that* He is a rewarder of those who diligently seek Him.
Hebrews 11:6

Another hindrance to receiving from God is a lack of faith. In Matthew 17:14-21 we read of Jesus' disciples not being able to cast a demon out of a child. As a result, he called them unbelieving, faithless and perverse. Jesus was not pleased with his disciples, but sounded rather exasperated with them.

Abraham, on the other hand, pleased God because he did not withhold his only son from him. He was ready and willing to obediently offer Isaac as a sacrifice, even though God had already told Abraham that all of his descendents would come from Isaac. By faith Abraham received Isaac and by faith he was ready to give him back to God. When Abraham was ready to go to the designated location and offer his sacrifice, he told his servants that **he and Isaac** would return after worshipping the Lord (Genesis 22:5). He did not say I will return.

As Abraham was preparing for the burnt offering his son asked him where the lamb was, to which Abraham relied, **"My son, God will provide for Himself the lamb for a burnt offering (Genesis 22:8)."** When Abraham was ready to slay Isaac, an Angel of the Lord intervened and provided a ram for the offering just as Abraham had professed.

Throughout his time of testing, Abraham showed **total unwavering and unquestioning trust in God**. For Abraham so loved God that he was willing to sacrifice is only begotten son. God would have never asked of Abraham what he himself was not willing to do. The day would come when God would offer his only begotten Son as a sacrifice for all the people of the world because of his unconditional love for them (John 3:16).

Do you want the faith of Abraham? The bible declares that faith comes by hearing

(Romans 10:17). Study the word, and quote the scriptures as much as possible. As you hear yourself saying God's word over and over, it will go down deep into your being, and your faith will begin to soar!

Wrong Motives

When you ask, you do not receive, because you ask with wrong motives, that you may spend what you get on your pleasures.
James 4:3 (NIV)

If you are not receiving, examine your motives. Are they selfish? Are they God-pleasing? King Solomon pleased God by asking for the wisdom to rule his people well. As a result King Solomon not only received great wisdom, but God also gave him tremendous riches. God also promised King Solomon a long life if he remained faithful in following his laws.

In James 1:5 we are told God will freely give us wisdom without criticism or blame. We just have to ask!

Unforgiveness

"And his master was angry, and delivered him to the torturers until he should pay all that was due to him.
So My heavenly Father also will do to you if each of you, from his heart, does not forgive his brother his trespasses."
Matthew 18:34-35

God freely forgives us and he expects us to do the same. Many of you are sick because you have given the torturers [demons] the legal right to inflict suffering upon you because you refuse to forgive.

Unforgiveness will keep God's best from you. Matthew 5:24 tells us to reconcile first with whomever you are angry with, and then bring your offering. The injustice imposed upon you may be severe, and the thought of forgiveness insurmountable, but you don't have to do it in your own strength. Ask God to help you. The act of forgiveness is for your emotional and physical healing. It is not to condone the wrong that was inflicted upon you. It is for your benefit. You will

---

never be able to move forward if you continue to harbor unforgiveness.

You may also be racked with guilt because you cannot forgive yourself for something you said or did. Paul referred to himself as a chief sinner (I Timothy 1:15) for killing Christians, but because of his conversion, he was able to boldly say that he had wronged no one (II Corinthians 7:2). He knew he was a new creation (II Corinthians 5:17). You too can have a fresh start by confessing your sins and receiving God's forgiveness.

If we confess our sins, He is faithful and just to forgive *our* sins and to cleanse us from all unrighteousness.
I John 1:9

Forgive and move forward with your life!

Having a Judgmental Spirit

"Judge not, that you be not judged. For with what judgment you judge, you will be judged; and with the *same* measure you use, it will be measured back to you.
Matthew 7:1, 2

Only God is the Righteous Judge. He sees the whole picture. We simply aren't qualified to judge. We don't have the whole story. Quite often when we judge someone it is because we see something in them that reminds us of something that we do not like about ourselves.

When the scribes and Pharisees brought the woman caught in the act of adultery to Jesus, they wanted to stone her for her sin. Jesus did not tell them not to stone her, but to ask themselves if they were without transgression. Realizing that they themselves were guilty of sin, they left one by one (John 8:3-9).

Therefore you are inexcusable, O man, whoever you are who judge, for in whatever you judge another you

condemn yourself; for you who judge practice the same things.
Romans 2:1

Because you reap what you sow (Galatians 6:7), you will receive judgment if you are criticizing others. If you want to be blessed, start by blessing others.

Possessing the Spirit of Fear

"And the Lord, He is the One who goes before you. He will be with you, He will not leave you nor forsake you; do not fear nor be dismayed."
Deuteronomy 31:8

Even though the topic of fear was addressed earlier in this book, it warrants additional discussion because fear is probably the biggest hindrance to receiving of all.

You are called to be a giant killer. That is what David did (I Samuel 17:49-51). No sooner had Samuel anointed David King of Israel, David was facing his giant. **Do not be surprised if you are suddenly facing your giant (problem) after going to a new level in your life.** Undeterred by Goliath's immense size (verse 4), he boldly proclaimed the giant's demise. He knew God was with him, and even though Goliath was a feared and evil Nephilim— a fallen angel human hybrid (Genesis 6:4), David knew his God was bigger.

David had such confidence in his God that he picked up five smooth stones because he was ready to take on Goliath's brothers as well (II Samuel 21:15-22) if he needed to. David was an expert marksman with his slingshot, so when he released the stone, it shot out of his sling like a bullet out of a sniper rifle, and subsequently sunk into Goliath's big fat head.

David used his faith in God and his unique gift to fell a Giant. David did not rely on Saul's gift of armor. It simply did not fit him, and actually would have slowed him down and would have worked against him. **Instead, David used the gift that God gave him to kill Goliath.**

What ever giants may have come your way to keep you from living your dream, like David, use your faith in God and your unique God-given gift to destroy the giant(s) in your life. You must realize that fearfully talking about your problems is not going to make them vanish. David, unlike the Israeli Army, did not talk about how impossible the task of defeating Goliath was going to be. Instead, he ran head-on towards Goliath, boldly glorified his God, declared Goliath's certain demise, and then proceeded to destroy him.

You may feel that your problem is as immovable as a mountain. The thing is mountains are movable (Zechariah 14:4). In the natural they are moved by the sifting of the tectonic plates, giving rise to earthquakes. In the spiritual, you blast them with the dynamite of God's word. In Matthew 21:21b Jesus said, **"but also if you say unto this mountain, 'Be removed and be cast into the sea,' it will be done."**

God would not give you a dream without fully equipping you, thus enabling you to achieve it. Do not adopt the fearful "grasshopper mentality" of the Israelites, merely existing and wandering in circles your whole life, and then sadly perishing without fulfilling your destiny (Numbers 14:26-38).

David was fearless because God was with him (I Samuel 16:13). If you have been born again (John 3:3), God is in you (John

17:11), and since God is love (I John 4:8), you have nothing to fear because perfect love casts out fear (I John 4:18).

Negative Words

The impact of negative words is discussed in part four of this book.

PART FOUR

The Reality of the Invisible

Believing Before Seeing Is Key

**For we walk by faith, not by sight.
II Corinthians 5:7**

Thomas would not believe that Jesus had risen from the dead unless he could see and touch where the nails had pierced his hands, as well as feeling Jesus' side where the roman solider had stabbed him. He walked by sight and not by faith.

Many people operate in the same manner. They say, "Unless I see with my own eyes, I will not believe." This is a limiting mindset because there is so much more to this universe than what our physical senses tell us.

Visible light, which we see with our own eyes, is only a very small part of the electromagnetic spectrum.[xiii] For example, we cannot see infrared and ultraviolet light, or X-rays and Gamma rays. These are invisible to us, but they exist. Our physical eyes simply do not see everything that is around us.

In like manner our physical ears cannot pick up all sounds. For example, a dog can hear a dog whistle just fine, but we cannot hear it at all. Does this mean the dog is crazy and hearing a sound that is not there. Or course not. This sound wave is simply out of our range of hearing.

The story of Elisha and his servant Gehazi in II Kings 6:15-17 is a good example of not being able to see something even though it is really there. When Gehazi awoke and went outside and saw that Elisha and he were surrounded by a Syrian army, he was understandably worried. He asked his master, "What shall we do?" To which Elisha, replied, "Do not fear, for those who are with us are more that those who are with them." Elisha then prayed that Gehazi's eyes would be opened. The Lord opened the young man's eyes and he saw that the mountain was full of horses and chariots of fire.

Even though we usually do not see them, there are angels all around us ready to help. Unfortunately there are also demons around us ready to do us harm as well. The saying, "What you don't know can't hurt you", is a dangerous lie. Hosea 4:6 states, "My people are destroyed for lack of knowledge." What you don't know **can** hurt you! To keep us from harm, is one of the reasons why the Holy Spirit gives us dreams and visions, or gifts like the word of knowledge, or the word of wisdom, but we have to ask him for these gifts.

Thoughts Are Real

"The Secret" claims that thoughts have a frequency, and as you think your thoughts are sent out into the universe.[xiv] They also claim that thoughts are magnetic and attract like things that are on the same frequency.

When Jesus forgave and healed a paralytic some of the scribes immediately said within themselves, "This man blasphemes!" Jesus, however, was able to somehow discern [tune into] the thoughts of the scribes as they reasoned among themselves. If, per chance, our thoughts are traveling through the cosmos, does it not make sense that they be good and productive thoughts?

But Jesus, knowing their thoughts, said, "Why do you think evil in your hearts?"
Matthew 9:4

Some scientists believe the thought process creates an electromagnetic field through the release of hormones and chemicals[xv]. If this theory is true, our thoughts do go out into the universe at the speed of light in the form of electromagnetic waves.

Electromagnetic waves are what make it possible for us to have radio broadcasts, satellite communications, navigational systems, computer networks, etc[xvi].

Perhaps we really are human transmission towers, although this cannot be claimed with complete certainty at the present time.

However, what is certain is that your thoughts do determine what you say and do.

"A good tree can't produce bad fruit, and a bad tree can't produce good fruit. A tree is identified by the kind of fruit it produces. Figs never grow on thorn bushes or grapes on bramble bushes. A good person produces good deeds from a good heart, and an evil person produces evil deeds from an evil heart. Whatever is in your heart determines what you say.
Luke 6:43-45 (NLT)

Neuroscience is the study of the nervous system. Included in this discipline is the study of the brain. **According to Dr. Leaf in her book, "Who Switched Off My Brain?"** during the thought process chemicals are secreted **to form the thought**. **Simplistically put,** if the chemicals are in the right proportions, your neurons (nerve cells) will look like healthy trees, and you will feel the good emotions like joy, love, peace, etc. If the proportions of the chemicals are out of balance, your neurons will look like diseased trees, and you feel the negative emotions like anxiety, depression, bitterness, etc.

Dr. Leaf explains, that since you are made in the image of God (Genesis 1:26) who **is love, and therefore** only thinks positive, negative thinking **uses the chemicals incorrectly upsetting the electrical chemical balance**. Negative thinking, therefore; will cause an imbalance within in the chemicals in your body. This in turn will lead to sickness and disease.[xvii]

God wants you to be healthy and whole. You can start to change your life by starting to think about what you are thinking about. Ask yourself, "Are my thoughts doing me any good?" Accept the good thoughts and reject the bad ones (II Corinthians 10:5). This is the way you start to renew your mind. By continuing this process you will put your life on the perfect path.

Don't copy the behavior and customs of this world, but let God transform you into a new person by changing the way you think. Then you will know what God wants you to do, and you will know how good and pleasing and perfect his will really is.
Romans 12:2 (NLT)

Words Have Power

"The Secret does not go far enough with law of attraction. It talks about having right thoughts, having faith, and performing the right actions, but it neglects to talk about the importance of words. God did not just think the universe into existence; he spoke it in to existence.

By the word of the Lord the heavens were made, And all the host of them by the breath of His mouth.
Psalm 33:6

Genesis 1:2 shows the Spirit of God hovering over an earth that is described as a dark formless abyss. We do not hearing God saying, "It is so dark and depressing out here. What a mess! I think it's getting even darker. This just is not going to work. I can't do this." Somebody get me a Prozac! No, He simply says, "Let there be light" and the light comes. In response to his voice, the light just doesn't trickle in. It reacts by screaming in at 186,000 miles per second! What a demonstration of His Awesomeness and, the power of words!

Since we are made in God's image (Genesis 1:26), our words are powerful as well. We always need to be mindful of what we say. Positive faith filled words that we speak will work for our benefit. Fear filled words that we utter will work against us.

Earlier I stated, "You can start to change your life by starting to think about what you are thinking about." You must apply this same principle to your words. Start thinking about the words you are saying. **Speak only, and I must repeat, positive, faith filled words!**

James 1:26 tells us that if you do not control your tongue, your religion is useless. And if your religion is useless, then your prayers will likely go unanswered.

There were times in my life when I felt like my prayers did not go past the ceiling. This is because I was the "Queen of Complaining". Even my prayers were one long whine and gripe session. No wonder they did not get answered. **God does not want to hear complaining from us, he wants us to agree with him.** We are told in Matthew 12:36 that we will be judged for every idle word we speak. Decide right now to agree with what God says in his word. Pray powerful faith filled prayers such as, **"I can do all things through Christ who strengthens me"** (Philippians 4:13). Do not pray negative fear filled prayers like, "Oh God, It's not working. I just can't do this." "I'm so fed up with everything." There is not one complaint in The Lord's Prayer! Stop harming your life with your grievances. God does not want your negative report. He did not receive it from the ten spies (Numbers 14:36, 37) and he's not going to receive from you. You are a child of the Most High God, and as his child you should imitate Him (Ephesians 5:1). Agree with what God's word says. Boldly and continually declare it over your life.

The Walls of Jericho Came Crashing Down

What are words if not but sound? Sound travels in waves and these waves can be destructive as well as creative. A tremendous example of how destructive sound waves can be is found in the sixth chapter of the book of Joshua.

As per God's instructions, forty thousand Israeli men of war (Joshua 4:13) and seven priests blowing shofars (rams horns) marched around Jericho once a day for six days. During these marches around the city, the men were not allowed to shout or even talk; the only sound made was that of the priests blowing the shofars. Since all matter resonates or vibrates, it is possible that during those marches the blowing of the shofars matched the frequency of the vibration of the walls which caused them to weaken.

On the seventh day they marched around the city in the same manner as the previous six days, but for a total of seven times. The people were also instructed to shout when the priests blew the shofars with a sustained blast. The result was that the walls fell down flat. This must have created a shock wave towards the already weakened walls. After all, the city had been marched around for a total of thirteen times and the walls subject to countless blasts of rams' horns!

Medical professionals are now using sound waves to break up kidney stones. This procedure is call lithotripsy. Extracorporeal shock wave lithotripsy (ESWL) is the most common type of lithotripsy. The high energy shock waves pass through a person's body until they hit the kidney stones. These sound waves break up the kidney stones into very small pieces which can then be eliminated from the body through the urine.[xviii] This example demonstrates the remarkable power of sound waves.

Cursing Words and Life-Giving Words

**Words kill, words give life; they're either poison or fruit—you choose.
Proverbs 18:21 (The Message)**

In Mark 11:12-14 we find Jesus cursing a fig tree for not having any figs, even though figs were not in season at the time. From the outset this appears quite odd. Why would Jesus be yelling at fig tree and telling it that no one would ever eat from it again? I wonder if his disciples thought he was losing his mind when they saw his outburst.

However, the next day it all became very clear. The fig tree was quite dead (verse 21). What Jesus had done was preach an illustrated sermon to his disciples on the extraordinary might of words.

Stop saying statements like, "This job is killing me! My children are driving me crazy!" "I'm so stressed out that I'm about to snap!" "My father had a heart attack at fifty and I'm probably going to have one too." You are harming yourself and jeopardizing your future.

An amazing demonstration of the power of words is in the account of Lazarus being raised from the dead (John 11:38-44). When Jesus arrived in Bethany, Lazarus had already been in the grave for four days. When Jesus told the disciples to roll away the stone, Martha promptly informed Jesus that there would be a quite a stench by now as her brother had been dead for four days. Jesus did not agree with her and say, "That is a big problem. Better leave the stone where it is." He did not lift up his eyes to heaven and say, "Father, we have a big problem here. Lazarus has been dead for four days and by now he stinks."

Does your problem stink? **Don't tell God your problem stinks; he already knows that!** Jesus simply said, "Father, I thank you that you have heard me (verse 41)." Jesus knew Lazarus was dead before he got to Bethany (verse 14). He had already prayed for the miracle that would take place. After thanking his Father, Jesus cried with a loud voice, **"LAZARUS, COME FORTH!"** Yes, the Holy Spirit was involved, but without Jesus commanding Lazarus to come forth, nothing would have happened. Lazarus would have remained dead.

If you want abundant supernatural life, pray and confidently speak the answer, **not the problem.**

The Tongue: A Weapon

And the tongue is a flame of fire. It is full of wickedness that can ruin your whole life. It can turn the entire course of your life into a blazing flame of destruction, for it is set on fire by hell itself.
James 3:6 (NLT)

The tongue is a fickle thing. We praise God with it and then turn around and curse people with it (James 3:9). My own father called me stupid more than he called me Doris. Even though I did well in school, I was a damaged individual severely lacking in confidence and self-esteem. This greatly impaired my ability to move forward with my life, and become the person that God intended me to be.

When I was growing up there was a saying that went like this, "Sticks and stones will break my bones, but words will never hurt me." The fact of the matter is that words do hurt. Proverbs 12:18 says [and I'm paraphrasing here] words can cut like a knife. This is exactly how I felt when my father called me stupid.

I like how Jabez dealt with the label he had been given. Despite his name meaning pain, he had the boldness to ask God to bless him, and to keep him from causing pain (I Chronicles 4:9, 10).

If you have been given a hurtful label, refuse to let it have dominion over your life. Someone may have used their tongue as a weapon against you, but you do not have to receive the evil words spoken over you.

Remember, the word of the Lord is also a weapon (Ephesians 6:17), and it can cut down any curse pronounced against you.

no weapon forged against you will prevail, and you will refute every tongue that accuses you.
Isaiah 54:17a (NIV)

The Gift of Tongues

On the Day of Pentecost, when the Holy Spirit fell on the believers in the upper room (Acts 2;1-4), we are told that what looked like tongues of fire settled on each of them. Unlike James' description of an evil tongue fueled by the fires of hell (James 3:6), these tongues were fueled by fire from heaven.

If you do pray in tongues, pray more. This gift is for your edification or benefit (I Corinthians 14:4). Paul said that he wished that all the believers in Corinth spoke with tongues (verse 5). He also stated that he spoke with tongues more than anyone there (verse 18). Paul allowed the Holy Spirit to pray through him, and I believe this greatly contributed to his amazing life.

Words have creative power. Let the Holy Spirit speak through you. Paul tells us in I Corinthians 12:31 to earnestly desire the best gifts, one of which is speaking with tongues. However, if you do not pray in tongues, or are not comfortable with the idea, quote scripture verses while you pray.   The important thing here is to agree with God's word when you pray.

PART FIVE

My Desire Manifested

My One Hundred Dollar Piano Stool with Bonus

**Delight yourself also in the Lord,
And He shall give you the desires of
your heart.
Psalm 37:4**

This is a true account from my own life on
how the law of attraction works. I have
wanted a piano since I was a little girl.
My father decided against the idea. He
said he had seen to many people invest
money in instruments and lessons only to
see their child give up music. I did not
understand the concept of being
persistent at the time, and so put the idea
out of my head. Whenever I did come
across a piano though, I would always be
attracted to it and start tinkering on it.

While visiting a friend in another part of
the country I started learning to play her
piano by going through some of the
lessons in her piano books. I was
smitten!

When I got home I bought an affordable
keyboard and some piano books and

proceeded to teach myself. I quickly outgrew the keyboard, but I did not have the money for a piano, but that did not deter me because all I **thought** and **talked** about was **"I want a piano!"** I started looking for a used piano in the classified ads. What I soon came to realize inexpensive pianos sold very quickly, nevertheless; I just kept on looking and believing for one.

One day an important though hit me; "I do not know how to by a good used piano, and I certainly do not want to wind up with a piece of junk or a costly repair bill." I went to the library and found books on how to buy a good used piano, and proceeded to educate myself.

One day my mother who lived in another part of the country sent me a cheque for one hundred dollars and told me to buy a treat for the whole family. A little while later I found two pianos advertised for sale in the local paper; one for five hundred dollars and one for one hundred dollars. I checked out the respectively priced five hundred dollar one first and found it needed a fair amount of repair. I then called the number advertising the one hundred dollar piano and got through on the first try, and yes it was still available, and yes I could come to see it right away.

When I arrived at the house I found out that the people selling the piano were going on a year long trip around the world, and the people to whom they were renting their house had their own piano. The piano was simply priced low to sell quickly. The amazing part was that I was the only one to get through on the telephone to enquire about the piano because they were selling and giving away so many other items that their phone was ringing off the hook!

Once in their house, I put my new found skills on how to buy a good used piano to work. As I was doing my inspection, the man selling the piano got a little nervous and told my husband that he would let the piano go for seventy- five dollars. This is kind of funny, because if you knew my husband, he loves to haggle, but he just said, "One hundred is fine."

After I decided to buy the piano, calls started coming in for it. This piano definitely had my name on it and it was in remarkable shape!

I tell people I bought a piano stool for one hundred dollars and they threw in the piano for free! Our mechanic came to help move the piano. Being a relatively light studio size model, the piano got a nice ride on its back in a pickup truck. The price: Ten dollars!

I owned that piano for eight years and did not put a penny into it. It just stayed in tune while I spent hours and hours playing it. When I finally decided to sell my piano because my family I and were moving across the country from Alberta to Ontario to spent time with my aging mother, I received seven hundred and fifty dollars for it. The buyer was a concert pianist who wanted a piano for his students. He graced us with several performances in our living room and the music was wonderful. He said the piano was only slightly out of tune and in very good shape. Awesome!

PART SIX

Becoming Reborn

You Too Can Have God's Favor

God wants to richly bless all of his children, and that includes you! No matter what you have done, forgiveness is available to you.

Before Ester was brought into the presence of the king for the first time she had to be pure—a virgin; she also had to be made presentable by undergoing twelve months of beauty treatments.

By making Jesus your Lord and Savior, you too can have access to God's presence because you are instantly made pure and presentable by being washed in his blood.

and from Jesus Christ, the faithful witness, the firstborn from the dead, and the ruler over the kings of the earth. To Him who loved us and washed us from our sins in His own blood,
Revelation 1:5

After Jesus gave up his spirit on the cross, the veil in the temple was torn in two from top to bottom (Mark 15:38). No longer was the Holy of Holies only accessible by the high priest. It was now open to all who would accept Christ's redemptive work on the cross.

Therefore, since we have a high priest who has ascended into heaven, Jesus the Son of God, let us hold firmly to the faith we profess. For we do not have a high priest who is unable to empathize with our weaknesses, but we have one who has been tempted in every way, just as we are—yet he did not sin. Let us then approach God's throne of grace with confidence, so that we may receive mercy and find grace to help us in our time of need. Hebrews 4:14-16 (NIV)

The Sinner's Prayer

For if you confess with your mouth that Jesus is Lord and believe in your heart that God raised him from the dead, you will be saved. For it is by believing in your heart that you are made right with God, and it is by confessing with your mouth that you are saved.
Romans 10:9, 10 (NLT)

The best thoughts you will ever think are:
Jesus is my Lord and Savior.
And the best words you will ever say are:
Jesus is my Lord and Savior.

Jesus said, "I am the way, the truth, and the life. No man comes to the Father except through me (John 14:6)."

If you have never asked Jesus into your life and you feel the Holy Spirit tugging at your heart strings right now, please pray the following prayer:

Jesus please forgive me for all of my sins.
Thank you for dying on the cross for me.
Please come into my heart.
I make you my Lord and Savior.
Amen.

If you prayed the above prayer and meant it with all of your heart, you are now born again, and there is much rejoicing in heaven right now over your decision.

"Likewise, I say to you, there is joy in the presence of the angels of God over one sinner who repents."
Luke 15:10

Your next step is to find a bible-believing church where you can fellowship with other believers, and where you will be taught the Word of God. In this way your faith will increase, and you will really start to believe that **with God all things are possible!**

Summary

Under extreme circumstances, **Job kept his integrity and believed** his redeemer lives and that he would see God (Job 19:25, 26).

By unwavering faith and trust in God, one hundred year old Abraham being as good as dead (Hebrews 11:12) became the father of a great nation.

Jacob went to work and used the resources that he had on hand (Genesis 30:37) to multiply his herds.

Joseph used **his God-given gift to interpret Pharaoh's dreams** (Genesis 41:25-32, 40) to step into his destiny.

David killed Goliath (I Samuel 17:50). He promptly dealt with the problem, while everyone else just talked about it.

Even though, David had opportunity to slay King Saul on two separate occasions (I Samuel chapters 24:11 & 26:23), **David waited for God's perfect timing** before taking the crown.

After wandering the desert for forty years, eighty-five year old **fearless Caleb** received his inheritance (Mount Hebron) and **drove out the giants** (Joshua 15:14).

Queen Ester found favor with the king **by fasting, and by wisely spending time with him** (Ester 5:6; 7:2) before exposing Haman's evil plot.

Gideon went on to subdue his enemies by **abandoning his negative grasshopper mentality. He came to believe what God said about him:** That he was a "might man of valor" (Judges 6:12).

Steps to Take

1. Ask, be specific, don't override another person's will; don't ask with wrong motives
2. Visualize, believe, feel, claim by faith, live in expectation, have a strong desire, persist in thinking positive despite obstacles
3. No doubting or wavering allowed; be focused
4. Your words should be in agreement with your desires; they too, have creative power
5. Your actions should mirror your desires
6. Show gratitude; give thanks
7. Exercise patience
8. Be a cheerful giver
9. Receive and give forgiveness
10. Don't be critical and jealous of others

Conclusion

After searching the scriptures, I believe the law of attraction works within the confines of God's sovereignty. Basically, this law is the sowing and reaping principle which God set in place, and how it operates is as follows: You **reap what you sow** (Galatians 6:7, 8).

The law of attraction works for everyone just like the law of gravity. Gravity keeps you from floating off into outer space, but if you jump off a cliff you are going to go **SPLAT!** Electricity is another good example. With electricity you can turn on a light at night, and read a good book [like this one; at least I hope you liked it!], or you can stick your finger in a light socket and get **ZAPPED!** It doesn't matter whether you believe in these laws or not. These laws can work to your advantage or they can work against you. It's your choice.

If you find yourself being upset because you see immoral people prospering, but you yourself are struggling. Perhaps it is because they are applying the laws that

God set in motion properly. They know what they want, and they go after it with **single-mindedness, persistence and determination.**

...for He makes His sun rise on the evil and on the good, and sends rain on the just and on the unjust.
Matthew 5:45b

If you are going to succeed in life you must use the law of attraction to your advantage, being very careful about the thoughts that you think, and the words that you speak. Make sure your actions are in harmony with your thoughts and your words, and remember:
Whatever you give out, be it good or evil, comes back to you!

Additional Verses to Speak and Meditate On

Zechariah 4:7
Matthew 6:33
Matthew 7:7, 8
Luke 12:32
John 14:13, 14
John 15:7
John 16:24
I Corinthians 14:2
II Corinthians 9:6
Ephesians 3:20
Philippians 4:6
Philippians 4:19
I John 4:16
I John 5:14

Notes

Recommended Reading

The Fourth Dimension; Dr. Paul Yonggi Cho; Logos International; Plainfield, New Jersey; 1979

Battlefield of the Mind; Joyce Meyer; Harrison House; Tulsa, Oklahoma; 1995

How To Live Like A King's Kid; Harold Hill; Logos International; Plainfield, New Jersey; 1974

The Tongue—A Creative Force; Harrison House; Tulsa, Oklahoma; 1976

The Dream Giver; Bruce Wilkinson; Moultnomha Publishers; Sisters, Oregon; 2003

Who Switched Off My Brain; Dr. Caroline Leaf; Thomas Nelson Publishers; Nashville, Tennesse; 2009

It's Your Time; Joel Osteen; Free Press; New York, New York; 2009

Cure for the Common Life; W Publishing Group, a Division of Thomas Nelson, Inc.; Nashville, Tennessee; 37214

Reposition Yourself; Living Life Without Limits; T.D. Jakes; Atria Books, a Division of Simon & Shuster, Inc.; New York, New York; 10020

Linking Procedures

Many websites do not allow deep linking. These instructions will take you to the particular pages I visited while researching this book.

http://www.nasa.gov/home
Type electromagnetic spectrum in search bar and click on the link that says Electromagnetic Spectrum – Introduction - Imagine the Universe

http://www.unisci.com
Type conscious mind into search bar and click on the link that says Our Conscious Mind Could Be An Electromagnetic Field

http://www.drleaf.com
Click on thought life in navigation bar

http://www.wikipedia.org
Type radio waves into search bar

http://www.surgeryencyclopedia.com
Type lithotripsy into search bar and click on the link that says Lithotripsy – procedure…

About the Author

Doris Rose Beerwald has been a Christian since 1984. Since that time she has studied the bible, read countless books, and listened to many, many sermons.

It is Doris' sincere desire to encourage, and inspire people to move forward with their lives, so they can go to the next level.

She currently resides in Toronto, Ontario, Canada with her family.

You can visit her website at **www.abundantsupernaturalliving.com**

Endnotes

[i]Byrne, Rhonda; The Secret; Atria Books; New York, New York/Beyond Words Publishing; Hillsboro, Oregon; 2006; page 164

[ii]Byrne, Rhonda; The Secret; Atria Books; New York, New York/Beyond Words Publishing; Hillsboro, Oregon; 2006; page 168

[iii]Byrne, Rhonda; The Secret; Atria Books; New York, New York/Beyond Words Publishing; Hillsboro, Oregon; 2006; pages 89-91

[iv]Byrne, Rhonda; The Secret; Atria Books; New York, New York/Beyond Words Publishing; Hillsboro, Oregon; 2006; page 46

[v]Byrne, Rhonda; The Secret; Atria Books; New York, New York/Beyond Words Publishing; Hillsboro, Oregon; 2006; page 27

[vi]Byrne, Rhonda; The Secret; Atria Books; New York, New York/Beyond Words Publishing; Hillsboro, Oregon; 2006; page 142

[vii]Byrne, Rhonda; The Secret; Atria Books; New York, New York/Beyond Words Publishing; Hillsboro, Oregon; 2006; page 79

[viii]Byrne, Rhonda; The Power; Atria Books; New York, New York; 2006; page 129

[ix] Byrne, Rhonda; The Secret; Atria Books; New York, New York/Beyond Words Publishing; Hillsboro, Oregon; 2006; page 128

[x] Byrne, Rhonda; The Secret; Atria Books; New York, New York/Beyond Words Publishing; Hillsboro, Oregon; 2006; page 107

[xi] Byrne, Rhonda; The Power; Atria Books; New York, New York; 2006; page 166

[xii] Byrne, Rhonda; Byrne, Rhonda; The Secret; Atria Books; New York, New York/Beyond Words Publishing; Hillsboro, Oregon; 2006; pages 113-114

[xiii] http://www.nasa.gov/home

[xiv] Byrne, Rhonda; The Secret; Atria Books; New York, New York/Beyond Words Publishing; Hillsboro, Oregon; 2006; page 10

[xv] http://www.unisci.com

[xvi] http://www.wikipedia.org

[xvii] http://www.drleaf.com

[xviii] http://www.surgeryencyclopedia.com

www.ingramcontent.com/pod-product-compliance
Lightning Source LLC
Chambersburg PA
CBHW060510030426
42337CB00015B/1823